God's
Amazing
Grace

Terry Virgo

ChristianLife
Books
TOOLS FOR SPIRIT-LED LIVING
ORLANDO, FLORIDA

Creation House
Strang Communications Company
600 Rinehart Road
Lake Mary, FL 32746

Originally published by Word UK in Great Britain in 1992.

CONTENTS

INTRODUCTION

For many of us, excitement over the grace of God is puzzling. We can remember the joy and release we experienced when we were born again, but now our Christian life has settled down, and we have lost much of our enthusiasm for God's grace.

"I've received His saving grace," you say, "and I want people to put their trust in God. But I don't know anything about the *riches* of His grace. What are the riches of God's grace anyway? Am I missing out on something?"

Sadly, many believers *are* missing out, but they do not realize it because they have never heard about the depth of God's grace and how it affects them. They live apparently normal Christian lives, but secretly they feel that they are fighting a losing battle. If they were honest, they would admit that they are often bored with their Christianity. God's grace, His free undeserved favor, was exciting once, but now — well, now life is almost mundane, and grace applies only to those who have not yet trusted Christ to save them, or so many believers think.

The truth is almost too good to be true! God's grace is so amazing that Christian teachers are often too nervous to declare it fully. They fear that if believers really grasp how freely God loves them, they will live carelessly and take advantage of that grace. To prevent this from happening, these teachers make sure they add a number of provisos to the message of grace — an action which actually obscures its transforming power.

There is a very real danger in the message of "free grace." It could lead to irresponsible and even sinful living. Peter addresses that fact when he says, "Live as free men, but do not use your freedom as a cover-up for evil" (1 Peter 2:16). But if we add the warnings too quickly, we shall muffle the sound of the good news and blunt the edge of its power to deliver.

Many Christians are too quick to add disciplines to the message of grace. Before new believers have ever understood that God loves them unconditionally, they add, "But, of course, you must always...and you ought never to...." The result is often that Christians simply believe that God loves them if they are good. We are back to salvation *by* works, not salvation *that* works.

This is not to say that Christian discipline is unimportant. On the contrary, the apostle Paul, who decries every hint of legalism, also calls us to godly discipline — a discipline which is not based on the legalistic hopeful search to earn God's blessing, but which is based on the faith that what God says is true of us.

We must follow Paul's example. Though he formerly persecuted the church of God, he received and gloried in the free grace of God, declaring, "By the grace of God I am what I am, and his grace to me was not without effect. No, I worked harder than all of them — yet not I, but the grace of God that was with me" (1 Cor. 15:10). Clearly, there is no tinge of legalism in all his hard work.

My prayer is that as you read *God's Amazing Grace*, God will grant you a richer enjoyment of the fullness of His salvation. May it be a life-transforming experience for you! May God reveal the truth about His grace to you and set you free to enter into a brand new relationship with Him!

ONE

REIGNING IN LIFE

*The trouble is that most Christians think
they're saved by grace but grow by sweat.*[1]
Stephen Brown

We "reign in life." "We are more than conquerors." "He always leads us in triumph." You read these truths in the Bible, and they strike a chord in your heart.

Yes, you think, that's my calling. That's what I'm meant to be — on top, reigning in life! Then you look at your experience and are filled with discouragement. That's where I *should* be, you think.

You recall times when you were stirred to make fresh endeavors to reign in life. There was that conference. God really touched you, and you resolved to do better for Him. Or there was that memorable New Year's Eve when you turned your attention on the clean, unmarred year ahead and decided, This one's going to be different. This time I'm really going to reign!

Maybe you set spiritual targets for yourself: I'll get up earlier; read the Bible in twelve months; pray harder; and witness to one person every week.

For the first few days you did quite well. Then you overslept and missed your prayer time. The following morning you had to read a double portion of Scripture which meant that you didn't have time to pray for as many individuals as you should have. By the end of the week you were trailing by eleven chapters and twenty-three people — but you had at least witnessed to the postman!

Since then your spiritual behavior has gone up and down. You gaze enviously at those who seem to sail through with God, and you hang your head and wonder, If I'm supposed to be a conqueror, why am I such a loser? Why do circumstances always seem to overwhelm me? Why don't I experience complete victory over temptation, sin and condemnation?

There are countless discouraged believers like you. They too hear the Scriptures about living in victory, and they too fail miserably to keep up their spiritual activities. Reigning in life is a great calling, they think. But it is more like a far-off mountain peak — beautiful yet unattainable.

A Different Gospel

Most of us have been taught from the early days of our Christian life that prayer, Bible study, fellowship and evangelism are what you ought to do if you want to be right with God. We assume, therefore, that once we have received salvation as a free gift, we then reign in life by working hard at these "rules."

Sadly the rules do not liberate — they imprison. We follow them a while, then we get behind, fall into condemnation and eventually end up in defeat.

Have you ever wondered whether striving to please God is the way to reign in life? The Galatians thought they could reign by keeping various rules. Having received salvation as a gift they were now trying to please God "by human effort" (Gal. 3:3). They were "observing special days and months and seasons and years" (4:10).

Other believers may have been impressed by these self-imposed rituals. Paul was horrified. "You foolish Galatians!" he rebuked them (3:1). He realized that they were putting themselves back under a system of law (4:21).

Others may have argued that they were just developing a slightly different emphasis. Paul said, "You...are turning to a different gospel" (1:6).

We may not realize it, but like the Galatians many of us have turned to a different gospel. Quite rightly, we receive salvation as a free gift. Quite wrongly, we try to reign by working hard at various rules.

If Paul were here, he would gaze at us in disbelief and cry, "You foolish Christians! Don't you realize that reigning in life has nothing whatever to do with your accomplishments? It's about what Christ has already accomplished for you. It concerns not what you do but what you receive. You reign in life when you 'receive God's abundant provision of grace and of the gift of righteousness' " (Rom. 5:17).

Grasp this truth, and it will totally liberate you!

———————

Jesus wants you to be a victorious Christian.

We are more than conquerors through him
who loved us (Rom. 8:37).

**Jesus wants you not just to be saved by grace,
but to continue in it.**

Therefore, since we have been justified through faith,
we have peace with God through our Lord Jesus Christ,
through whom we have gained access by faith
into this grace in which we now stand (Rom. 5:1-2).

TWO

MR. LAW
OR MR. GRACE?

*If you do not see Law being honored on the cross
of Calvary, you have never seen the true meaning of the
death of Christ: it is essentially an honoring of the law
...and because the law has been honored in that way
we are now free to be married to the Lord Jesus Christ.*[1]
Martyn Lloyd-Jones

Are Christians under the law or not? How you answer this question will have a bearing on the way you live. The pious Jews of Jesus' time thought that salvation was obtained through meticulous observance of the law. By "law" they meant not only the old covenant commands given to Moses, but a large number of additional laws as well. These extra regulations had sprung up from their interpretation of the law. Thus they tithed not only their incomes, but their mint, dill and cummin as well (Matt. 23:23).

As we read the New Testament, it becomes increasingly apparent that the Pharisees were totally bound by the demands of the law. This fact is most clearly evident in their encounters with Jesus.

Today unbelievers think that Christians are people who are just as locked into rules as the Pharisees were. They reason that with this being the case, it would be better to enjoy life now and become a Christian when they are older and need God more.

An Imperfect Husband

Paul responds by giving us an illustration. He tells us that mankind is the wife of a husband called Law (Rom. 7:1-6). Mr. Law is an austere figure who has complete authority over us. Day after day we live under his condemnation: You're wrong! Stop this! Don't do that! He points out our shortcomings but never lifts a finger to help. To make matters worse, we can't argue with him because we instinctively know that he is always right.

Mrs. Law may say that she wants Christ to be her husband, but she cannot marry Him because she is already married and would be committing spiritual adultery (Rom. 7:2-3). To paint the picture totally black, the law will never pass away (Matt. 5:18). We are permanently married to an overbearing, fault-finding, unhelpful husband — and he will never die.

What's the solution? We have "died to the law through the body of Christ" (Rom. 7:4). When Jesus died on the cross, He took away the curse of the law.

At our conversion we were placed into Christ and were crucified with Him. The law didn't die. We did! Christ fulfilled all the demands of the law, and we have been totally released from its power.

Our freedom from the law can be likened to a soldier's discharge from the army. For a time the young recruit is subjected to harsh military training. Then one day he is discharged. When his sergeant sees him strolling carelessly across the parade ground, he is horrified and barks out the order to stand at attention.

At first the recruit cringes, but then he remembers that this man no longer has any authority over him. The sergeant can scream and yell as much as he likes, but he has no control over someone who has been discharged.

The answer to the question "Are Christians under the law?"

is no. The law is designed for those who have not been born again. We are no longer under its power. Although the law may continue to make endless demands on us, we are dead to it (Gal. 2:19). "Christ is the end of the law...for everyone who believes" (Rom. 10:4).

A Perfect Husband

We were not discharged from the law to do our own thing, but so that we "might belong to another" (Rom. 7:4). That person is Jesus.

There is a vast difference between the two husbands. Mr. Law was harsh and overbearing. He wearied us with his demands yet offered us no help.

By sharp contrast, Jesus is gentle and humble in heart. He gives us rest for our souls, an easy yoke and a light burden (Matt. 11:29-30). Our old husband gave us rules. Our new one gives us love.

Jesus, the bridegroom, left His heavenly Father and earthly mother to be united to His bride. He proved His love for us through His agonizing death on the cross to win us. His Father approves of His Son's choice of bride and confirms that we were chosen in Him before the creation of the world (Eph. 1:4).

We could not have a better husband. He shares His life with us and showers us with spiritual and material blessings. He listens to us and intercedes with His Father on our behalf. He lets us work alongside Him now and has made wonderful plans for us in the future. We are joined to Jesus "in order that we might bear fruit" (Rom. 7:4).

We could not do this when we were under the law because the law is incapable of imparting life. If the law had been able to make us fruitful, then righteousness would have come by the law (Gal. 3:21). The law would have said, "Do not covet," and on hearing the words we would have been released from all covetousness immediately.

But the law can only say that something is right or wrong and condemn us in the process.

Whereas the law is impotent, Christ is fruitful. At the beginning, God wanted Adam and Eve to "be fruitful and increase in number" (Gen. 1:28). That blessing of fruitfulness now rests on Christ and the church.

Jesus' words are spirit and life (John 6:63). The marriage is consummated when we first receive His Word and become Christians (John 15:3). As we live intimately with Jesus and obey the Word, God answers our prayers (John 15:7), and Jesus completes our joy by making us fruitful.

Spiritual Adultery?

Christians have one husband, not two. Most of us may understand this in theory but are often unaware of it in practice. Let me illustrate.

Bob is not a Christian, but he knows a believer named Phil and is impressed by him. He's different, Bob thinks. There's something wholesome and joyful about him.

God begins moving in his heart. Bob's first resolve is to clean up his act, so he meets with other Christians and tries to be like them. He wants desperately to do better, but he actually feels worse because he keeps failing. Then one day he hears the gospel and realizes that he cannot work his way into God's favor. He goes to the counseling room and is gloriously saved.

But almost before he has had the chance to enjoy his new-found freedom, some devoted believer says, "Right, now you're a Christian, you must read the Word and pray every day and you mustn't do this or that, and...." No sooner has he escaped from the law and its demands than he is plunged into arduous religious laws.

As he goes through the Christian life, he meets other believers who are also struggling to keep these exhausting rules — and failing. They share the same feelings of condemnation.

Then Bob is in a worship meeting, and God speaks to him, saying, "I love you. I justified you. I'm for you."

Bob feels like the prodigal son. "Oh, thank You, Lord!" he says. "I receive Your grace and love. I want to come back to

You." Then he adds, "And this time I won't let You down. I'll read my Bible every day and I'll...!"

Many of us have fallen into the same terrible trap as Bob. We have been set free from the demands of our old husband but are vulnerable to feelings of condemnation from him. To get rid of these negative feelings we try to please our new husband by working harder at the very rules that our old husband had required of us! This is spiritual adultery, and it can't work.

Our relationship with Christ is not based on law but on grace. We do not gain greater acceptance with God by "cleaning up our act." We have been discharged from the law. It has no power to condemn us, and we must never submit to it again.

Jesus gave His life to fulfill God's commands for you.

Do not think that I have come to abolish the Law
or the Prophets; I have not come to abolish them
but to fulfill them (Matt. 5:17).

Jesus wants you to see Him as a life-giving husband.

I have come that they may have life, and have it
to the full (John 10:10).

The letter kills, but the Spirit gives life (2 Cor. 3:6).

Jesus wants you to stand in grace.

For the law was given through Moses; grace and truth
came through Jesus Christ (John 1:17).

THREE

What's the Use
of the Law?

*"This is the covenant I will make with the house
of Israel after that time," declares the Lord. "I will put
my law in their minds and write it on their hearts. I will be
their God, and they will be my people...I will forgive
their wickedness and will remember their sins no more."*
Jeremiah 31:33,34b

S ince we are no longer under the law, we will be forgiven
for wondering if it accomplishes anything. Where does it
fit into God's plan?

The Law Reveals Sin

Society tends to live by its own standards of right and wrong.
Each individual simply acts as far as his particular conscience
will allow. By contrast, God's law provides us with absolute
standards about what is acceptable and what is not. Paul says, "I
would not have known what coveting really was if the law had
not said, 'Do not covet' " (Rom. 7:7). When we covet, we sin,
and when we sin, we break the law (see 1 John 3:4).

The Law Provokes Sin

Let's say that it is a beautiful, sunny day, and you have decided to visit a park. You put the dog in the car, and when you arrive you discover that dogs are not allowed in the park. Your immediate reaction is to rebel against the rule: My dog is perfectly well-behaved. I don't see why he shouldn't come in with me. Besides, I'll keep him on a leash.

You stroll along the path for five minutes before you notice a number of signs along the path. They remind you: DO NOT WALK ON THE GRASS. Until you saw the signs, you probably had no intention of walking on the grass; but as soon as you became aware of the rule, you actually found yourself wanting to disobey it. Sin lay dormant until it was provoked. Then something in you reacted to the desire to sin. This is the sense behind the words, "But sin, seizing the opportunity afforded by the commandment, produced in me every kind of covetous desire" (Rom. 7:8).

Most people are quite happy to believe in God. "Yes," they say, "there must be a Maker behind it all somewhere. I go to church sometimes...."

But if you tell them God says they shouldn't do that, their whole attitude changes, and they become hostile. They are fine until the law intrudes. Then the law provokes them, and they react.

The Law Leads Us to Christ

In the Greek culture there were slaves whose job it was to take the children to school. Using this analogy, Paul tells us that "the law was put in charge to lead us to Christ" (Gal. 3:24). The law was designed to condemn unbelievers and to steer them to Christ, who will save them and cause them to reign in life.

Paul says that the "law is made...for lawbreakers and rebels" (1 Tim. 1:9a). God's law will drive people to Christ — which is why we must keep preaching it in our evangelistic endeavors. Believers are not under the law. When Paul was discussing sexual immorality, he did not point to the Ten Commandments. He argued not from law but from grace: "The body is not meant for sexual immorality, but for the Lord, and the Lord for the body" (1 Cor. 6:13b). He was consistent. We must be consistent too.

A Totally New Deal

Legalistic Christians are trying to live a New Testament life in an Old Testament way. This is impossible because the two covenants are entirely different and affect people in totally different ways. The old covenant was given to Moses on Mount Sinai. When he came down the mountain he found that the Israelites were worshipping a golden calf. Livid with anger, he smashed the tablets on which the Ten Commandments had been written and ordered the Levites to execute judgment. They killed about three thousand people in a single day.

The new covenant was given to the disciples through the Holy Spirit at Pentecost. When Peter came from the upper room, he accused the people of an infinitely worse crime than idolatry. They had crucified the Lord of glory. Surely God would inflict a dreadful punishment on the murderers of His only Son. But what happened? God poured out His grace, and about three thousand people were saved in a single day. That's glorious revenge from heaven!

The two covenants are totally different. The old covenant was written on stone (Ex. 31:18). It emphasized obedience to the law and brought judgment and condemnation. The new covenant is inscribed on hearts (Heb. 8:10). It focuses on the free gift of grace and brings mercy and release. For Christians, the old covenant is obsolete (Heb. 8:13) because it has been superseded by a better, more glorious alternative (2 Cor. 3:9). The old covenant emphasized performance, and it judged us. Then Christ came, and His performance completely satisfied the Father. When we trusted Jesus to save us, we were relying on Him to fulfill the demands of the law for us. The new covenant emphasizes position. Through the cross Jesus has lifted us into a reigning position. God has seated us with Him in the heavenly realms

(Eph. 2:6) and has accepted us in the One He loves.

This is a new deal. God wants us to know this since it will affect our relationship with Him and with others.

The Pharisees had an attitude which said, "Are you keeping the rules as well as I am?" This bred competition and robbed them of fellowship.

The early church refused legalism, "and much grace was upon them all" (Acts 4:33). Let's stop striving to impress God and instead live in the good of what Christ has done for us.

Jesus wants you to live by faith in Him.

Everyone who sins breaks the law; in fact,
sin is lawlessness (1 John 3:4).

But Israel, who pursued a law of righteousness,
has not attained it. Why not? Because they pursued
it not by faith but as if it were by works
(Rom. 9:31-32).

Jesus longs for your friendship.

The Lord would speak to Moses face to face,
as a man speaks with his friend (Ex. 33:11a).

You are my friends if you do what
I command (John 15:14).

FOUR

CHRISTIANS: SINFUL OR RIGHTEOUS?

*"Christ in you, the hope of glory." I'm not afraid of
the devil. The devil can handle me — he's got judo I
never heard of. But he can't handle the One to whom
I'm joined; he can't handle the One to whom I'm united; he
can't handle the One whose nature dwells in my nature.*[1]
A. W. Tozer

E arlier I asked the question: Are Christians under the law?
Then, with the help of the Scriptures, I answered no.
Now I'm asking another question: Are Christians
righteous?

You remember the verse, "There is no one righteous, not even
one" (Rom. 3:10). And you decide that except for Jesus Christ,
"the Righteous One" (1 John 2:1b), everybody is basically sinful. That's true of me, you think. I'm just a sinner who does a
few righteous acts now and again.

Next morning you doze through the alarm and get up late.
Someone else has used all the hot water, so you start the day in
a bad mood. You try to pray, but you can't stop your mind from
wandering. You open your Bible at the day's reading from Levi-
ticus and discover that it's all about cleansing from mildew! You
give up on that too. At breakfast time you spill the milk onto the

table and vent your rage on the cat. As you storm off down the street, the devil whispers in your ear, "Righteous? Never! There's no righteousness in you at all."

His voice lingers in your ears all day. "You're useless!" His accusations wear you down, and everything you do seems to turn out wrong. You become superstitious, concluding that it's all because you didn't have a decent quiet time. In the evening you look back over a hopeless day and feel thoroughly condemned. Even when you're having excellent times with God, you still can't seem to win.

"I really made some progress this morning," you say.

"That's true," says the devil. "Doing well, aren't you?"

"Yes," you reply.

"You're quite proud, aren't you?" he continues.

You wonder how you will get through.

Joshua, the high priest, once came before God. He was wearing filthy clothes, which were symbolic of sin. Satan was ready to condemn him, but God silenced Satan before he could utter even one word against Joshua. Then He took away Joshua's sin and clothed him in fine garments (Zech. 3:1-5).

We are "a royal priesthood" (1 Pet. 2:9), and Satan accuses us "day and night" (Rev. 12:10). He often does this to stop us from bringing our priestly offering of worship to God. But whereas God silenced the devil, we often prefer to listen to him instead of to God! His accusations against us sound so accurate. We know how badly we fail. We feel wretched about it but conclude that we've simply got to live with the condemnation and do our best under the circumstances.

In Adam

Let's answer the question of whether or not Christians are righteous by starting at the beginning and looking first at the man whose unrighteousness we inherited.

We read that "Adam...was a pattern of the one to come" (Rom. 5:14b). He was a "type of Christ." We see many other "types of Christ" in the Scriptures. Joseph, the favorite son, became ruler in the land of Egypt and rescued his family from death. Moses was a great shepherd who led his people out of slavery. Even Noah's ark typifies Christ. All who were in it were saved.

These and many other examples tell us about Christ. We might be surprised to see Adam in the list since he is known, more than anything else, for his sin. But he typifies Christ in that what he and Christ did affects the whole human race.

Concerning Adam, we read, "Sin entered the world through one man, and death through sin, and in this way death came to all men, because all sinned" (Rom. 5:12). When Adam sinned, I sinned. I do not remember sinning in Adam, but God put his sin to my account and judged me guilty. I was born sinful and had a strong built-in tendency to sin.

When you are locked into Adam, you can never justify yourself, but you might try to do so. One day you might decide, I'm going to turn over a new leaf and be nice to people. So you help some little children cross the road, and you go shopping for your neighbor. You send a card to someone who's going through a difficult time and invite a friend to stay for a weekend. You even start going to church and praying. Then you look over your accomplishments and think, I'm doing quite well.

Your good deeds have undoubtedly helped others, but there's only one problem — you're still *in* Adam.

When we are in Adam, "all [not some of] our righteous acts are like filthy rags" (Is. 64:6). It doesn't matter how good or religious we are; we will never justify ourselves before God. It has nothing to do with touching up our lives here and there. It's about a radical new start. We must get out of Adam. We must be "born again" (John 3:3).

In Christ

Just as Adam is the head of one race of people, so Christ is the head of another totally different race.

The effect of their actions on us is clearly stated in Romans 5:18: "Just as the result of one trespass was condemnation for all men, so also the result of one act of righteousness was justification that brings life for all men."

When we are born again, a radical change takes place. We are taken out of Adam and placed in Christ. A glorious illustration of this transaction is found in the Old Testament. Isaac and Rebekah had two sons: Esau and Jacob. When Isaac was old he wanted to bless Esau, whom he loved more than Jacob. He told Esau to go out, hunt wild game and prepare him some tasty food. After Isaac had eaten he would bless his son. But while Esau was out, Jacob put on his brother's clothes, pretended to be Esau and stole the blessing (Gen. 27). Jacob clothed himself in Esau. He hid in the favorite son's identity and approached his father.

That's what happens to us. We hide ourselves in Jesus and approach the Father. But there is a difference: Jacob went trembling to Isaac hoping that he would not be found out.

We, however, are not hiding by our own cunning. God has accepted us and placed us in the Son He loves. Jacob stole Esau's blessing, but God has "blessed us in the heavenly realms with every spiritual blessing in Christ" (Eph. 1:3b).

God does not want us to fear that He will find us out, because the closer we get to Him, the more He will catch the fragrance of the Son He loves. If you are a Christian, you died, and "your life is now hidden with Christ in God" (Col. 3:3). Whereas once your association with Adam condemned you, now your association with Christ justifies you (Rom. 5:16). You are in Christ, and if anyone is in Christ, he is not a sinner: "He is a new creation; the old has gone, the new has come!" (2 Cor. 5:17).

As Martin Luther says, "Christ took our sins and the sins of the whole world as well as the Father's wrath on His shoulders, and He has drowned them both in Himself so that we are thereby reconciled to God and become completely righteous."

Jesus is victorious over the devil.

And having disarmed the powers and authorities, he made
a public spectacle of them, triumphing over them
by the cross (Col. 2:15).

**Jesus wants us to understand that we are saved
not by works but through faith in Him.**

A man is justified by faith apart from observing
the law (Rom. 3:28).

God...has saved us and called us to a holy life — not
because of anything we have done but because
of his own purpose and grace (2 Tim. 1:8-9).

God is on your side.

Therefore, since we have been justified through
faith, we have peace with God through
our Lord Jesus Christ (Rom. 5:1).

God was pleased to have all his fullness dwell
in him, and through him to reconcile to himself
all things...by making peace through his blood,
shed on the cross (Col. 1:19-20).

FIVE

JESUS, OUR RIGHTEOUSNESS

*It is in the Lord that men are justified; it is in
the Lord their righteousness resides;
the Lord Himself is their righteousness.*[1]
John Murray

Under the old covenant, an individual bringing a sacrifice to the priest was not concerned about his own appearance. He didn't worry that the priest would see the tear in his coat or the spot on his tunic. His eyes were on the lamb. While the priest inspected it, the man would wonder if his offering was acceptable. Would the priest find something wrong with it? Was it good enough for God? Would it atone for his sin?

When he returned the lamb to its owner, the priest would say, "I find no fault in this man" (Luke 23:4, KJV), and all heaven agreed.

Jesus is "a lamb without blemish or defect" (1 Pet. 1:19). He has fully satisfied the Father on our behalf. Trying to add any personal righteousness to Christ's sacrifice in order to make it more acceptable to God is therefore pointless. Something which is already perfect cannot be improved.

This is why we can "approach the throne of grace with confidence" (Heb. 4:16). We are confident not in ourselves, but in the One who gave His life for us.

"Yes," you say, "I realize that I can't do anything to save myself, but surely God accepts me only if I continue to do righteous things." No! You must understand that you *are* righteous. Righteousness, like salvation, is a free gift. Those who reign in life "receive God's abundant provision of grace and of the gift of righteousness" (Rom. 5:17b).

Paul was once "as for legalistic righteousness, faultless" (Phil. 3:6). He thought that he had to work at being righteous — until he became a Christian. Then he turned his back on all his strivings and wanted to "be found in him [Christ] not having a righteousness of my own that comes from the law, but that which is through faith in Christ — the righteousness that comes from God and is by faith" (Phil. 3:9).

Righteousness comes free with Jesus! Just as Adam made you sinful, so Christ makes you righteous. You are not righteous some of the time, but always. Jesus is "the same yesterday and today and forever" (Heb. 13:8). When God looks at you, He sees the glorious righteousness of His Son and declares, "I find no fault in you." And all heaven agrees.

Cure for Condemnation

Earlier in this book we examined the wretched state of trying hard to be righteous but failing miserably.

We saw how in that state you felt wretched about the way you continually failed the Lord and concluded that there was nothing to do but put up with the sense of condemnation and work harder.

You are struggling to rid yourself of the guilt and condemnation associated with "not doing well enough." Next day you do better and feel quite pleased with yourself — until you hear that Mrs. Jones prays for three hours a day and fasts every Tuesday! Condemnation doesn't diminish; it increases. You can never quite do enough.

What's happening here? You feel condemned because you are focusing on your performance. You think you're accepted because of what you do. In other words, you are trying to overcome condemnation with sanctification, which is impossible.

There is only one answer to condemnation: justification. You cannot be condemned and justified at the same time. If the judge declares you to be not guilty, there's no condemnation.

You are accepted because of what Christ has already done. It has nothing to do with how you feel or what you do, whether you fell asleep during your prayer time or fasted for a week. Jesus has released you from the law, justified you and given you His righteousness as a gift.

There is no way that you can make yourself either more or less righteous. You are in Christ Jesus, and there is no condemnation for you (Rom. 8:1). You thought you couldn't win. The truth is: you can't lose!

Paul questions, "Who will bring any charge against those whom God has chosen? It is God who justifies. Who is he that condemns?" (Rom. 8:33-34a). The accuser is the devil. He is active day and night (Rev. 12:10b) and will do all he can to rob you of your security in God. He will constantly bombard you with accusations about your poor performance and attempt to force you into a treadmill of dead works.

Martyn Lloyd-Jones has expressed it thus:

> The Christian should never feel condemnation; he should never allow himself to feel it. The devil will try to make him feel it; but he must answer the devil. If the devil comes to you and tries to convict you, and to make you feel that you are condemned, stand up to him and say, "There is therefore now no condemnation to them which are in Christ Jesus." Answer him with the Scripture, and he will "flee from you."[2]

"Resist him, standing firm in the faith" (1 Pet. 5:9a). You have an advocate with the Father who always lives to intercede for you (Heb. 7:25; 1 John 2:1).

GOD'S AMAZING GRACE

Grace Be With You

I can hear you say, "But hold on a minute. If Christ is my righteousness, then I can sin and still be righteous! I can be thoroughly horrid, push my way to the front of the bus line, get angry with people and fail to pray for three months — yet I will remain righteous in Christ! The grace of God seems to give me full permission to sin. The more I sin, the more I will prove the greatness of God. That's the most dangerous teaching I've ever heard!"

Yes, it is. Martyn Lloyd-Jones says that if our gospel never provokes the question of whether we shall carry on sinning, then we are probably not preaching the gospel at all.

But Paul's gospel forces you to think, If I'm righteous anyway, why don't I sin happily from now on?

The answer to the question comes very fast: "By no means" (Rom. 6:2). The King James Version renders it, "God forbid," and J. B. Phillips translates it, "What a terrible thought!"

We will look into this a little more later on. For now I want you to dwell on God's amazing grace.

When I was at school I used to paint watercolor landscapes. Once I had painted a blue sky I could not immediately add a brown and green tree because the colors would all run into one another and make an awful mess on the paper. But if I waited until the blue had dried, then I could continue painting.

We must have a clear grasp of grace before we begin painting on it. Later God may want to teach us various disciplines: intercession, fasting and prayer, but none of them has to do with reigning in life.

If we add them too quickly, we are in danger of losing hold of grace and returning to the false belief, "God loves me if I'm good." Paint that way on your life, and you will make an awful mess!

So live with grace for a while. Let the truth about it set you free. God loves you unconditionally with an everlasting love. He has made you totally and eternally righteous through faith alone. You reign in life when you "receive God's abundant provision of grace and of the gift of righteousness" (Rom. 5:17).

———————

We are made righteous in Christ.

But...a righteousness from God, apart from law, has been
made known...This righteousness from God comes through
faith in Jesus Christ to all who believe (Rom. 3:21-22).

Jesus was condemned in your place.

The people of Jerusalem and their rulers did not recognize
Jesus, yet in condemning him they fulfilled the words
of the prophets that are read every Sabbath (Acts 13:27).

I tell you the truth, whoever hears my word and believes him
who sent me has eternal life and will not be condemned;
he has crossed over from death to life (John 5:24).

God wants you to be strong in grace.

And the God of all grace...will himself restore you and
make you strong, firm and steadfast (1 Pet. 5:10).

SIX

PROCLAIM FREEDOM

All my life I have been seeking to climb out of the pit
of my besetting sins, and I cannot do it, and I
never will unless a hand is let down to draw me up.[1]
Seneca

Pam and Bill are among many believers who have been set free by the truth concerning God's grace. Here are their true stories, with Pam relating hers first.

"It was a continual struggle to keep the law, and the inevitable failure produced guilt and condemnation. I felt doomed to a life of never quite making it. When I first heard about grace and freedom from law, the news was almost too good to be true. I realized that God accepted me totally, just as I was; that He loved me through and through; and that He gave me His righteousness so I didn't have to try hard to produce my own. Guilt and condemnation melted, and I relaxed and accepted myself.

"When I sin, I can now cope and find forgiveness quickly. This has meant that I am a softer person, less critical and more tolerant of myself and others, and able to forgive easily. God's grace stops me from writing myself off when I blunder. Life is busy, but I am no longer an uptight, self-righteous and miserable sort of person. God has benefitted too! Whereas before I was bored in His company, I now enjoy Him so much! I worship Him with abandonment and revel in His presence."

Then Bill gives his story: "I reasoned that to establish the kingdom, I would need to demonstrate my commitment by *paying the price*. Included in this price were authority, submission, obedience, discipline, correction and sacrifice. After several years of living by these principles I began to feel burdened by them. They put me under pressure to perform, and if I didn't consistently live up to the expectations of others, I felt like a failure. Slowly I lost my peace and joy, and it began to occur to me that something was missing in my life. People seemed happier without God than with Him. Surely if they found more excitement in a sinful world, why should they join me in saving it?

"When I discovered that God loved me unconditionally, I realized that I no longer had to strive to earn His or anyone else's approval. My acceptance wasn't based on my ability, so I didn't have to complete a list of requirements in order to have fellowship with Him. The grace of God brought renewed peace and joy to my life. I once saw my family as a burden, but now I view them as co-workers and enjoy spending time relaxing with them. I'm so excited that I have not been called to dead works but to serve a living God!"

Slaves of Sin?

Knowing the truth about grace sets us free, but it does not give us license to sin. Having understood who we are in Christ, we do not take advantage of God's grace—we live in the strength of it. God has not called us out of law and into sin. He has called us to be holy — not through our own endeavors, but through what He has done for us in Christ.

The dilemma that most Christians seem to face seems to be not so much "Shall I go on sinning?" but "If only I could stop sinning."

The Israelites once lived in slavery in Egypt. On the night of their deliverance God saw the blood that they had put on their door frames and passed over them. Their sins were covered by the blood of the lamb. They were saved. But as they tried to move forward, their slave masters pursued them, and the Red Sea blocked their progress into full liberty.

This is where some Christians live — between Egypt and the Red Sea. They know that they are forgiven, but their slave master, Sin, is constantly in hot pursuit. They repeat and confess the same sins again and again and hang their heads in defeat. "I'm locked into these things," they say. "There's no escape."

There is an escape. The Red Sea opened up. The Israelites went through it and stood on the other side. The slave masters followed, and the water flowed back and wiped them out. "Not one of them survived" (Ex. 14:28b). The Israelites were not simply forgiven; they were totally released. Christians have been "buried with [Christ] through baptism into death" (Rom. 6:4a). They have not only been declared righteous but delivered from the power of sin. You can be free from sin.

Now you say, "That's very nice, but you don't know the grip sin has on my life. How does this work out in practice? Should I be seeking a death-to-sin experience? Or should I just 'let go and let God'? What must *I* do, and what is God's part?"

Don't You Know?

Jesus said, "You will know the truth, and the truth will set you free" (John 8:32). A knowledge of the truth is the starting point to being released from sin. God is doing some remarkable things these days. Christians are having mighty encounters with Him and are doing extraordinary works for Him. I praise God for every new experience and for the zeal and commitment of His people. But I sense that Christians are in danger of seeking experiences or relying on experiences or willpower to set them free. We are not released through experiences or willpower but by knowing the truth.

John frequently uses the words "we know..." in his epistles, and Paul uses the phrase "Don't you know...?" In Romans 6:3 he says, "Don't you know that all of us who were baptized into Christ Jesus were baptized into his death?" Here he is questioning our understanding of our identity in Christ. How we perceive ourselves drastically affects the way we live.

When the Israelites arrived at Canaan, Moses sent out twelve leaders to spy out the land. On their return, ten of them reported that although the land was very fruitful, the enemy was far too strong. "We seemed like grasshoppers in our own eyes, and we looked the same to them," they said (Num. 13:33b). They couldn't press into the land and win it because they had already concluded, "It's hopeless. We're losers."

Bondage was all they had known in Egypt. For years they had no possessions, no promotion, nothing to give them any sense of self-worth. "Carry this," they were told. "Do that."

Then one day God not only delivered them from slavery, but He also allowed them to plunder the Egyptians (Ex. 12:36). He was saying, "I'm not just rescuing you. I'm giving you back your dignity."

The problem was that although they were out of slavery, slavery was not out of them. They peered into the promised land and declared in despair, "We can't possibly go in there. We're grasshoppers."

Many of us are like that. "I'm just a slave of sin," we say. "I've always been mastered by this. It's been going on for years. I can't help it." We see ourselves as slaves.

But this is not true. "Don't you know that all of us who were baptized into Christ Jesus were baptized into his death?" says Paul. Don't you know your identity? If you want to be free from sin, you must change your perspective about who you are.

Dead to Sin

God does not see three races on planet Earth: in Adam (sinners), in Christ (righteous) and in Christ but messing around with sin! Either we are in Adam, or we are in Christ. There is no middle position. It is not true to say that some exceptional

Christians have had a death-to-sin experience and that all other believers should seek this experience in order to be set free. The Scriptures make it clear that everyone who is in Christ has been crucified with Him (Rom. 6:6; Gal. 2:20). If we have been united with Him in His death (Rom. 6:5), we have also been freed from sin (Rom. 6:7).

Do you realize that God says that you have been crucified with Christ? You might protest that if God knew about your bad temper or your unclean imagination, He would not say that your old self had been crucified. It seems very much alive! But this is where faith must play its part. We do not remember dying with Christ any more than we recall sinning in Adam. We simply believe the Bible when it says that what happened to them is accredited to us. When we understand that we were included in Jesus' death to sin, we shall actually experience freedom from sin. All Christians have already been "baptized into Christ" and are already dead to sin.

This does not mean that baptism renders sin powerless over us. Some years ago people used to teach that if you had a sin problem, it was probably because you had not been baptized properly. So they would repeatedly baptize Christians to help them overcome their sin.

The trouble is that baptism symbolizes burial, and you do not bury people in order to kill them! You bury them because they are already dead. When they buried Jesus, it was final proof that He was dead. We are dead to sin because of our union with Christ. We are not "being crucified" with Him. It's a past event (Gal. 2:20). When He died, we died; when He was raised up, so were we. All that He accomplished is ours.

When God took us out of Adam, He did not revamp our old nature. He gave us a brand-new one — the divine nature (2 Pet. 1:4). We are not forgiven sinners but are new creations. "The old has gone, the new has come!" (2 Cor. 5:17b). Jesus is the new foundation in our lives.

At this point I should like to point out that the New International Version of the Bible uniquely and unhelpfully translates the word *flesh* as "sinful nature" (Gal. 5:13). You will naturally have to battle against fleshly desires, but you will never have to strive to overcome your sinful nature because you do not need to hold down something that is already dead!

Maybe you are thinking, He doesn't know me. I wish my thought-life really were dead. It's absolutely screaming with life!

Well, either you believe God, or you don't. We agree that two men were crucified with Christ because this is what the Bible says. We have no other proof. That same Bible tells us that "our old self was crucified with him" (Rom. 6:6). God, who is the truth, says that this is the truth. Do you believe it?

You are God's son (or daughter), not His slave.

Because you are sons, God sent the Spirit of his Son into
our hearts, the Spirit who calls out, "Abba, Father."
So you are no longer a slave, but a son; and since you are a
son, God has made you also an heir (Gal. 4:6-7).

There is deliverance through God's power.

[God] is able to do immeasurably more than all we ask or
imagine, according to his power that is at work within us
(Eph. 3:20).

God wants you to know that you have died with Christ.

I have been crucified with Christ and I no longer live,
but Christ lives in me. The life I live in the body,
I live by faith in the Son of God, who loved me
and gave himself for me (Gal. 2:20).

SEVEN

TOTAL LIBERTY

*The Christian life is not stumbling along, hoping to
keep up with the Savior. He lives in me and I live
in Him. And in this identification with Him, His power
becomes mine. His very life becomes my life
guaranteeing that His victory over sin is mine to
claim. I no longer need to live as a slave to sin.*[1]
Charles Swindoll

So often we are tempted to water down the truth. The devil whispers to us, "You ought to be free from sin, but you're not really. You're under its power, totally condemned."

The interpretation of Romans 7:14-25 has bewildered many Christians. How can Paul be wretched and incapable of doing good one minute, and the next be declaring freedom from condemnation and victory for every believer? How can he wish churches "grace and peace" when he is in such turmoil? How can he exhort the Philippians to rejoice (Phil. 4:4), when he is so miserable? What then are we to make of this?

Paul had already told us that the law both increases sin and kills us (Rom. 7:5,13). Now he takes this man — any man — and uses him to reveal the law's complete inability to save, justify or sanctify us. The man in the passage is under intense conviction of sin. The Spirit has shown him the holiness of the law, and he has suddenly become aware of his own weakness and inability. Rather than receive the grace of God, he thinks that he must struggle to keep the law in his own strength. The battle that ensues leads him into frustration, condemnation, despair, bondage and ultimate failure. "And that," says Paul, "is what the law will do for you if you try to keep it" (see Rom. 7:23).

This truth came home to me very vividly some years ago. Although I was a Christian, I used to be eaten up with jealousy toward someone. I hated the feeling but somehow I couldn't seem to master it. Then one day while reading Romans 6, I came to verse 7 which says, "Anyone who has died has been freed from sin." Suddenly the truth hit me.

Of course, I thought, a corpse never feels jealous or angry or self-pitying. You can be very rude to it, and it won't be offended or answer you back. It's dead, so it's freed from sin. So great was the impact of this revelation that I laughed out loud! My relationship with the person I envied has been excellent ever since. The truth set me free.

To overcome in any area of your Christian life you must start by knowing the truth and then by acting on what you believe. That is exactly what Abraham did when God told him that he would be a "father of many nations" (Gen. 17:5). On hearing the news, Abraham could have said, "Lord, You must be joking. A hundred-year-old man with a barren wife cannot produce one son, let alone a multitude!" But he held onto God's promise and saw in Isaac the beginning of its fulfillment.

You can say, "Lord, You don't know me," and argue with Him. Alternatively, you can submit your life to the truth. God's confident assessment is this: You have died with Christ; you are a radically transformed being; you have total liberty from all bondage to sin.

Start Counting

God says that we have died to sin. The first step is to believe that what He says is the truth. The next step is to "count" ourselves dead to sin on a daily basis (Rom. 6:11). The word *count* or *reckon* in this verse is an accounting term which tells us to "put it in that column because it goes there." Paul is telling us to consider the truth and live by it.

I am not preaching the power of positive thinking. We do not scrunch up our faces and think our freedom into reality.

This came home to me very forcefully when I was on an aircraft to Spain. As we touched down, the pilot informed us that it was 4:00 P.M. But my watch told me he was an hour fast. I could have thought, He doesn't know what he's talking about. It's 3:00 P.M. Then I might have decided, Well, maybe I'll force myself to believe he's right. It's 4:00 P.M.! It's 4:00 P.M.! I know it's 3:00 P.M.! No, it's 4:00 P.M.! The reality was that *in Spain* it was 4:00 P.M.

When you move from one nation to another, you often change time zones and need to adjust your watch to the reality of your situation. When you move from Adam to Christ you enter a sphere which is totally free from sin's power, and therefore you need to adjust your thinking to the truth. The truth is that as a slave to sin, you needed releasing. Jesus alone releases captives from their sin.

There was a day when He walked into the slave market, looked around and saw you standing there — filthy, in chains and under sentence of death. Then He pointed to you, said, "I'll take that one," and paid the top price for your life. He bought you from sin's control. You are no longer a slave to sin. You are a slave to righteousness. You have a totally new Master. Have you grasped this? Believe it because it is true. It's what God says.

In Watchman Nee's words:

> The more I reckoned that I was dead to sin, the more alive I clearly was. I simply could not believe myself dead, and I could not produce the death....one morning...I was upstairs sitting at my desk reading the Word and praying, and I said, "Lord, open my eyes!" And then in a flash I saw it. I saw my oneness with

Christ. I saw that I was in Him, and that when He died I died. I saw that the question of my death was a matter of the past and not of the future, and that I was just as truly dead as He was because I was in Him when He died....I was carried away with such joy at this great discovery that I jumped from my chair and cried, "Praise the Lord, I am dead!" Oh, it was so real to me! I longed to go through the streets of Shanghai shouting the news of my discovery. From that day to this I have never for one moment doubted the finality of that word: "I have been crucified with Christ."[2]

Do Not Let Sin Reign

Paul says, "Do not let sin reign in your mortal body so that you obey its evil desires" (Rom. 6:12). The body is the only part of us that has not yet been redeemed. This aspect of our salvation is still in the future. Paul says that in the meantime we "groan inwardly as we wait eagerly for our adoption as sons, the redemption of our bodies" (Rom. 8:23b).

When you were a sinner in Adam, your old nature and your body were in agreement to sin. Sin expressed itself through your body. You looked at, touched, heard and said things that were sinful. It was an unholy alliance which you were powerless to control.

Now your old sinful nature has been replaced by a new righteous nature. But sin is looking for somewhere to reign in your body. First it comes to the door as temptation, asking to enter in.

"Knock, knock," it says. "I've got something here that you can't resist!"

We see the sin we want, open the door, indulge in the goods and later regret our action. Soon our consciences become dull. The process of entertaining the sin continues until he moves in as a semipermanent lodger. It is not long before that lodger is reigning as the master of the house.

You were once totally at the mercy of your sinful desires, but now your new nature gives you the power to deny your body

37

permission to sin. That is why Paul can say, "Do not let sin reign." There is nothing mystical about this. Paul tells us to put to death the things that belong to our earthly natures, then he nails down what he means: "sexual immorality, impurity, lust, evil desires and greed...anger, rage, malice, slander and filthy language" (Col. 3:5b, 8b).

"If only I could stop that," you say.

God replies, "You can. Stop it!"

"But I'm only human," you protest.

"Well," says God, "if you're 'only human,' you must be born again. If you're born again, you're not 'only human.' You have the divine nature and can live victoriously as a result of it."

The Christian who continues sinning is being foreign to his true nature. The one who questions whether God is able to subdue his flesh is doubting the great God who can open seas, smash down walls and feed multitudes. Christ is in you. His power is available to you. Use it.

**God wants you to know that you have
been freed from sin.**

Through Christ Jesus the law of the Spirit of life
set me free from the law of sin and death (Rom. 8:2).

Jesus wants you to think right.

Finally, brothers, whatever is true, whatever is noble,
whatever is right, whatever is pure, whatever is lovely,
whatever is admirable — if anything is excellent
or praiseworthy — think about such things (Phil. 4:8).

EIGHT

A WILLING
SACRIFICE

The temptation once yielded to gains power. The
crack in the embankment which lets a drop or two
ooze through is soon a hole which lets out a flood.[1]
Alexander MacLaren

Paul says, "I urge you...in view of God's mercy, to offer your bodies as living sacrifices, holy and pleasing to God" (Rom. 12:1). This is not a cold command: "Surrender your bodies!" It is linked with the amazing love of God. Paul is saying, "In the light of God's incredible mercy toward you, how can you do anything else but offer your body to Him?"

God is looking for people who will give their bodies to Him, but not out of obligation. Jesus was not compelled to lay down His life for us. He could have commanded thousands of angels to defend Him from a cruel death. But, seeing the joy that was set before Him, He willingly "bore our sins in his body on the tree" (1 Pet. 2:24).

Paul tells us, "You are not your own; you were bought at a price. Therefore honor God with your body" (1 Cor. 6:19b-20). The holy life is not automatic. Your will is involved. You have to choose whether you use your body as if it belonged to you or to God.

The Jews at the time of Malachi were offering God imperfect sacrifices. They withheld the perfect animals for themselves and gave Him the leftovers, thinking any old thing would do for Him. God rejected the sacrifices because they were not worthy of Him. "I am a great king...and my name is to be feared among the nations," He said (Mal. 1:14b).

Only the best is good enough for the Lord. The Father is no longer looking for dead animals but living sacrifices, not sloppy lives but instruments of glory and praise in the earth. Are you giving your best to Him? He will test you by your actions. He will watch you to see if you are really honoring Him with your body.

What sort of things are you looking at, listening to, saying and touching? How are you treating your enemies? What is your attitude at work? How are your relationships with other members of your family?

Sanctification has nothing to do with "handing your life over to God." It is about cooperating with Him as He brings things to light that He wants you to change. Jesus was the perfect living sacrifice. When you wholeheartedly offer your body to God, you are saying, "I want to demonstrate my love to You for all that You have done for me."

No!

Paul says, "Do not offer the parts of your body to sin" (Rom. 6:13a). This is a command that we can obey. God has energized us with a new life and has given us the authority to say no to unrighteousness.

"But," you say, "this particular temptation is simply too strong for me. I can't help yielding to it. I'm powerless." You are mistaken.

No temptation has seized you except what is common
to man. And God is faithful; he will not let you be

tempted beyond what you can bear. But when you are tempted, he will also provide a way out so that you can stand up under it (1 Cor. 10:13).

According to the Bible, such a temptation does not exist. If you have allowed sin to come in and reign, you are sinning by choice — because you like it, not because you cannot control yourself.

You have a similar attitude to the little boy who was getting ready to join his friends by the river. Before he left, his mother told him, "You mustn't go in the water."

"All right, Mommy," he said, and rushed out of the house with his bathing trunks and towel.

When his mother called him back she asked, "What are you doing with those? I told you not to go in the water."

"I know," he replied. "But if I see everyone else swimming and can't help myself, then I've got my stuff."

One day we will all stand before God in His holiness. When He asks us, "Was any temptation too great for you?" which of us will dare to say, "Yes, this one"? We will not argue our case before the God who has already said, "There is no temptation too great for you."

We will bow humbly and agree with Him, "No, Lord, there was no temptation too great for me."

If we are going to confess it then, why not boldly confess it now? "Lord, this temptation seems like a giant, and I feel like a grasshopper, but the reverse is true. I can overcome — not by my willpower but by faith in Your Word. You say that I have been freed from sin. I believe it, and I will act on that belief."

You have complete authority over your body. Refuse the devil's lie that says, "You'll never be free from that sin; it has a complete grip on your life." The battle against sin has already been won. Satan — not you — was the loser. So decide now to stop making provision for your flesh — putting yourself in situations where you might be tempted. Say to your feet, your eyes, your hands and your ears, "No! That's not for you. I died to sin and will not allow it to reign in my life anymore."

Winners

Some people think that Christians are basically sinful. "We're like onions," they say. "We're clothed in Christ's righteousness, but if you peel off all the layers, you eventually find a rotten sinner."

This belief is utterly foreign to the Bible. In fact, quite the opposite is true. People who are born again are basically righteous. No matter how many layers you peel off, you always find a righteous son.

Am I teaching sinless perfection? Not at all. I am saying that sin is out of character for the Christian. John says, "No one who is born of God will continue to sin, because God's seed remains in him; he cannot go on sinning" (1 John 3:9). Indeed, John's reason for writing the letter was "so that you will not sin" (1 John 2:1). He expected Christians not to sin, then he added, "But if anybody does sin." In other words he was saying, "If anyone is foolish enough to sin." If we confess our sin, there is mercy. But we do not need to sin in the first place.

Imagine a large building with great steps leading up to a magnificent front door over which are the words, *That you will not sin*. At the back of this beautiful building is a fire escape over which is written, *But if anybody does sin*. Normally we walk in and out of the front door. Sometimes, however, we are silly and sin. Then we come in at the rear, confess our sin and find immediate forgiveness from God.

The tragedy occurs when Christians think that the normal way in and out is via the fire escape. "I'm just a sinner," they say. "Just a beggar telling others where to find bread."

That is not the gospel. If we are beggars, we are still grasshoppers in our own sight — which is not true. The Bible says that "we are more than conquerors through him who loved us" (Rom. 8:37). Christian, you are not a grasshopper — you're a conqueror. Not a sinner but a winner! Get rid of all grasshopper thinking. It is inappropriate for those to whom God "gives...the victory through our Lord Jesus Christ" (1 Cor. 15:57b).

Billy Graham has said that "the strength for our conquering

and our victory is drawn continually from Christ. The Bible does not teach that sin is completely eradicated from the Christian in this life, but it does teach that sin shall no longer reign over you. The strength and power of sin have been broken. The Christian now has resources available to live above and beyond this world. The Bible teaches that whosoever is born of God does not practice sin. It is like the little girl who said that when the devil came knocking with a temptation, she just sent Jesus to the door."[2]

Jesus wants you to exalt Him in your body.

I eagerly expect and hope that I will in no way be ashamed, but will have sufficient courage so that now as always Christ will be exalted in my body (Phil. 1:20).

Jesus wants you to resist temptation.

The grace...teaches us to say "No" to ungodliness and worldly passions, and to live self-controlled, upright and godly lives (Titus 2:11-12).

Jesus wants you to make a positive contribution to His kingdom.

The righteous are as bold as a lion (Prov. 28:1b).

NINE

HOLY
LIVING

*Many have ambitions which are never realized,
goals which are never reached, aspirations for
usefulness which are never fulfilled, visions which
never materialize. While the failure may at times be due
to limited ability, too often the deficiency is not in native
endowment but in character. The capacity for gruelling
application is lacking. There may be the promising start,
but not the discipline required to carry through.*[1]
Richard Shelley Taylor

God has said to you, "Be holy, because I am holy" (1 Pet.
1:16). Now if you are fundamentally a sinner, you will
have serious problems obeying this command. If an
eagle says to a pig, "Fly because I fly," that pig is going to have
a terrible identity crisis! If our hearts are basically sinful, how
can we possibly be holy? The command is a recipe for disaster.
It will thoroughly condemn us and will insure that Christians are
the most miserable people on planet Earth.

But the truth is that if you are a Christian you can "fly." God
has given you His divine nature. He has called you to holiness,
and you have the capacity to be holy, to live like Jesus and even
to be "more than a conqueror" through Him. Paul says, "Sin
shall not be your master" (Rom. 6:14). This is not an exhorta-
tion; it is a statement of fact. An incredible transformation happened when you stepped out of Adam and into Christ, from one

slave owner to another.

According to the Bible, all unbelievers are slaves to sin. They can be obvious sinners (murderers, rapists, burglars, drug addicts and so on) or respectable, good-living, churchgoing people who have never been born again. Because these individuals are slaves, they cannot simply walk free. They need releasing.

Paul says, "You have been set free from sin and have become slaves to righteousness" (Rom. 6:18). As it is only natural for righteous people to live righteously, "offer the parts of your body to [God] as instruments of righteousness" (Rom. 6:13b). By living righteously you are not striving to become righteous but are demonstrating that righteousness is already within you. By producing fruit that not only looks righteous but tastes of righteousness, you will prove that you are a slave of righteousness and will be useful to God.

The more you continue to live for God, the more you will discover the inherent righteousness working within you. Then you will find yourself turning away more and more from sin and moving forward in righteousness and victory. This is what Paul meant when he said, "Walk by the Spirit, and you will not carry out the desire of the flesh" (Gal. 5:16, NASB).

Sin will make you feel wretched and inconsistent with the righteousness that God is developing in you. That is why you feel awful when you sin. Your new master, Righteousness, is prodding you, saying, "Hey, slave! What are you doing? Get back into line." Live in the sphere where you feel most comfortable. It's called righteousness. Tune into your new master and be "filled with the fruit of righteousness that comes through Jesus Christ — to the glory and praise of God" (Phil. 1:11).

Ah, Discipline!

There are two extreme positions when it comes to the subject of discipline.

Matthew and Simon may both be Christians in the same church, but they have very different expectations in their day-to-day relationship with God.

Matthew has been taught that daily duties are extremely important if he wants to grow as a Christian. He therefore sets his alarm for 6:00 A.M. and gets up soon after it rings. He may be feeling like a piece of chewed string, but he refuses to let that deter him and rob him of the hour he *must* spend with God. Jesus expects me to follow His example, he says to himself.

Matthew reads through the Bible passage for the day, prays for the people on his prayer list and goes off to work. He hopes that he is impressing God as he replaces his desires for physical comfort — a cozy bed and extra sleep — with spiritual activities. The church leaders all know that he is serious about his relationship with God, and Matthew feels sure that God will bless him for his devotion.

Simon hates spiritual discipline! He rarely sets his alarm. If he does, the chances are that when it wakes him up, he will switch it off, turn over and go back to sleep! If he has had a particularly late night, he will not think twice about staying in bed until the last possible minute. I'm under grace, so I don't need to go through all those stuffy spiritual rituals, he thinks.

Simon happily involves himself in church activities and evangelism but has no time for anything which has the merest whiff of legalism attached to it. He does read the Bible and pray — but not on a regular basis. Spiritual endeavors like this can be done anywhere. They have to be fitted around his many other pursuits and frequently get left out altogether. The church leaders see Simon as an easy-going Christian, and he rejoices that he is free in Christ not to engage in rigid daily routines.

Although they might not realize it, neither of these individuals has understood the essence of discipline — neither Matthew nor Simon has it right.

Matthew thinks that he is disciplined when he is, in fact, bound by legalism. He has a superb relationship with his Bible and prayer list. But he would be taken off guard if you ever asked him to tell you about his relationship with Jesus.

This request would pose a problem. Although Matthew has a regular devotional hour, he rarely considers the quality of it. For him the overriding concern lies not so much in *enjoying Jesus' presence* as in *having a regular time*. The two are vastly different. If he were honest with you, Matthew would tell you that his devotional times are boring. He sees them as tasks that Christians should do and that good feelings are of secondary importance. "You have to get on with them" he affirms, "and just believe that God will reward you because He sees your secret devotion."

Simon, on the other hand, thinks that he is free from legalism when he is, in fact, at the mercy of indiscipline. He covers his tracks by being involved in all sorts of Christian activities, but he lacks depth of character and tends to be shallow in his understanding of God. He would feel uneasy if you asked him, "What has Jesus been saying to you recently?"

This question would present a problem because Simon never really spends long enough with Jesus to find out what He is saying. He rarely stops to ask if he is actually doing what God wants. Rather he assumes that if an activity seems right, then it is probably OK to engage in it.

If he were honest with you, Simon would tell you that behind the scenes, his Christian life is really something of an aimless mess. He does "Christian things" but has never disciplined himself to spend time working out the purpose and direction of his life. He muddles through, planning no definite goals. "You must be yourself," he says. "The early church did not have Bibles. They just lived from what they felt." Sadly he fails to realize that the early church was devoted to the apostles' teaching, told to treat doctrine very seriously and encouraged to guard the gospel which they had received.

Soldiers, athletes and farmers know only too well how important discipline is. Without it they would never have the stamina to fight, the strength to keep going or the goods to supply. Christians who serve God to their fullest potential are neither controlled by laws nor guided by feelings. They have learned the need for personal discipline.

Before his conversion Paul thought he would gain credit with God by striving to be righteous, so he worked hard at the law (Phil. 3:5-6).

When he realized that righteousness was a gift, he stopped trying to attain it by human effort, but he did not settle down into a cozy grace. "[God's] grace to me was not without effect," he said. "No, I worked harder than all of them — yet not I, but the grace of God that was with me" (1 Cor. 15:10). The hard work continued, but the motivation behind it was different.

Legalism speaks from outside and declares, "You've got to do this."

License is influenced by society and protests, "You don't have to do anything."

Discipline springs from within and says, "I want to do it." Are you disciplined?

Jesus wants to return for a beautiful bride.

Christ loved the church and gave himself up for her to make her holy, cleansing her by the washing with water through the word, and to present her to himself as a radiant church, without stain or wrinkle or any other blemish, but holy and blameless (Eph. 5:25-27).

Jesus wants you to be disciplined.

The sluggard craves and gets nothing, but the desires of the diligent are fully satisfied (Prov. 13:4).

TEN

ARE YOU IN THE WORLD, OR IS THE WORLD IN YOU?

It is right for the Church to be in the world;
it is wrong for the world to be in the Church.
A boat in water is good; that is what boats are for.
However, water inside the boat causes it to sink.[1]
                                    Harold Lindsell

When you grasp something of the wonder of God's grace, you realize how far away the world has drifted in its understanding of Christianity. Christians have almost unconsciously allowed the world to dictate its code of life to them. When the church adopts worldly practices, society is bound to come to the wrong conclusion about the nature of God's grace and about the true definitions of worldliness. Clearly, believers need to embrace a life-style and a way of thinking which accurately reflect the grace of God working in them. They must never give in to worldliness.

Worldliness

When Christians do not understand grace, they send a garbled message to the world. Society then looks at the church and concludes that Christianity is all about following a lot of rules and regulations. If we do not squelch this belief and promote the message of grace, we will open the church door to all sorts of worldly opinions and practices. God wants us to be a distinctive people who know that they have been set apart for His glory. Just as we received God's grace, so we must continue in it. If we see worldliness in the church or in our lives, we must be diligent to root it out. But first we need to know what worldliness looks like.

What people have done to avoid worldliness! The fourth century hermits withdrew from society and wandered around the desert pursuing lives of self-denial. They prayed, meditated, fasted, went without sleep and sometimes even walled themselves up in caves. The illiterate Simeon Stylites actually spent the last part of his life on top of a pillar in Syria, and Daniel, who followed him, spent thirty-three years on a column near Constantinople.

Even today in some Christian circles there is the feeling that to avoid worldliness you need to withdraw from society. So we see the establishment of Christian communities in ranches and farms in the countryside. The people in them pursue a self-sufficient and somewhat austere life-style — working on the land, eating its produce and emphasizing spiritual disciplines.

But Jesus never expected us to withdraw from the world. He prayed only that we would be protected from the evil one while we were in it (John 17:15). When John wrote about the "world," he was referring to the age in which we live. He was telling believers not to get wrapped up in a passing phase to which neither we nor Jesus belongs.

Some Christians think of worldliness in terms of obvious sins like cheating, lying, swearing and smoking. But worldliness runs deeper than that. It originates not in action but in attitude. A worldly Christian does not necessarily do blatantly evil things. He simply carries on without any particular reference to God, filling his mind with this age and living as though today were everything.

Society tries hard to control you, to "squeeze you into its own mold" (Rom. 12:2, Phillips). The apostle Paul realized that the New Testament Christians were living in great danger of allowing the world to control them. His concern extends to believers today. We are living under tremendous pressure to conform to the standards of society. God is calling us not to remove ourselves physically from worldly influences, but to resist that temptation to exclude Him from our daily lives.

What, according to the Bible, are the true roots of worldliness?

Worldly Wealth

Society declares, "Money is the answer for everything" (Eccl. 10:19). Jesus says, "You cannot serve both God and money" (Matt. 6:24b). Money has the power to corrupt. Fall in love with it and you may find yourself pursuing all kinds of evil. The world expects you to put yourself first. So when you are offered a promotion with a substantial salary increase, the world urges you to take it.

There is nothing wrong with a promotion, but if you take it only because you will be better off, you are basing your decision on money principles. Have you asked God what He thinks? Do your church leaders agree? If you do not accept the position, your colleagues may think you're crazy. But you do not belong to their kingdom. Isn't it more important to obey God than to do what others expect?

Worldly Wisdom

Worldly wisdom rebels against God's wisdom. Modern thinkers rule out "all that nonsense about Adam and Eve" and consider you crazy to pin your hopes on someone who was crucified nearly two thousand years ago.

"It's ludicrous to believe the stories of a group of fishermen and tax collectors," they say. "And the resurrection couldn't have been literal." The simple message of the cross is an insult to their intelligence. "Salvation cannot be a free gift," they say.

"We reach God by following the moral teaching and example of Jesus." Then they look at the church and declare, "You'll never attract people unless you make the way to God more acceptable to the modern man."

Today's intellectuals rebel against the Scriptures. "It's not sensible to believe and obey the Bible," they say. Humanly speaking, they are right. But they are judging its contents on the basis of logic. While they are working everything out rationally, God is doing His thing in a completely different way.

"We have conducted ourselves in the world," Paul says, "not according to worldly wisdom but according to God's grace" (2 Cor. 1:12). Whenever you face an issue, you choose whether you apply to it God's wisdom or man's foolishness. Faith rejects the sensible advice of men and puts total confidence in the Word.

Jesus was the most unworldly person who ever lived on earth. Did He withdraw from society? No. His mission was to reach people, and He could do that only if He mixed with them. "You are the light of the world," He told us. Our goal is to shine "before men," not to escape from them (Matt. 5:14-16).

> May I never boast except in the cross of our Lord Jesus Christ, through which the world has been crucified to me, and I to the world (Gal. 6:14).

The world offers only short-term success, so it is pointless to put any hope in it. Paul's boast was not in outward worldly things; it was in the cross. God wants us to have the same attitude. The world crucified Jesus, and the cross strikes a death blow to all our earthly aspirations. By taking up our cross (Luke 9:23) we are saying to God, "I'm laying down my life for You."

Satan lies to the world, offering its inhabitants an increasing number of physical pleasures. Jesus, who is the truth (John 14:6), wants us to turn away from worldly thinking and be sanctified by the truth (John 17:17). We must reject worldly thought patterns and live according to His Word.

God no longer wants to relate to us through external laws but through relationship. In the Scriptures He warns us to avoid certain major sins but does not give us a conclusive list.

So when we want to know whether it is OK to go to the theater or play golf on Sundays we need to ask, "Can I thank God for this? Is the peace of Christ ruling in my heart?" (Col. 3:15). His Spirit will tell us what He wants us to do.

The Bible tells us that "this world in its present form is passing away" (1 Cor. 7:31b) and that the "night is nearly over; the day is almost here" (Rom. 13:12). The night began when Adam sinned and all mankind fell with him. But now day is breaking into the darkness. Sinners will continue to live as if this world will never come to an end. It is senseless and out of character for sons of light to follow suit. Those who are righteous in Christ and who really do belong to an everlasting kingdom must "put aside the deeds of darkness and put on the armor of light" (Rom. 13:12). Go! And shine with heavenly light before men in worldly darkness!

Jesus wants you to follow Him wholeheartedly.

What good will it be for a man if he gains the whole world,
yet forfeits his soul? (Matt. 16:26).

God's wisdom and the world's wisdom are poles apart.

If any of you thinks he is wise by the standards
of this age, he should become a "fool" so that
he may become wise (1 Cor. 3:18).

**Jesus wants you to love Him more than
anything or anyone else.**

Whoever has my commands and obeys them, he is the one
who loves me. He who loves me will be loved by my Father,
and I too will love him and show myself to him (John 14:21).

ELEVEN

BATTLE FOR
THE MIND

Our voluntary thoughts not only reveal what we are;
they predict what we will become. Except for that
conduct which springs from our basic natural instincts,
all conscious behavior is preceded by and arises out
of our thoughts. Anyone who wishes to check on his
true spiritual condition may do so by noting what his
voluntary thoughts have been over the last hours or days.[1]
A. W. Tozer

Before we became Christians, we were blind, hard and hostile toward God. We needed revelation and transformation. We still need them today. As God reveals the truth to us, He wants us to allow Him to transform our wrong patterns of thinking.

If you tell someone he has just won a huge sum of money in a competition, he will be ecstatic!

In the days before he receives the prize, he will be telling everyone about it and working out exactly what he wants to do with it. "I'll take a vacation in the Bahamas, and I'll move to a bigger home and buy a better car...."

Now imagine that the day before the man is handed his longed-for check, he learns that there has been a mistake and he has not won after all. Devastated, he calls to find out what has happened. He is angry that the error was not noticed earlier and is resentful toward the man who got the prize. He sulks in self-pity and retreats to the local bar where he drowns his sorrows.

Influence a person's thinking, and you will always affect his reactions. That is why there is such a fierce battle for the mind. On the one hand Satan wants us to adopt negative thought patterns and live by them. On the other hand God encourages us to "take captive every thought to make it obedient to Christ" (2 Cor. 10:5b).

It took more than a new religion to translate Paul from a kingdom of darkness to a kingdom of light. He was forced to admit that he needed a devastating change of mind and heart, a great salvation which he could by no means work to attain.

A bit of churchgoing on Sunday and a few good deeds during the week may satisfy the human ego, but they do nothing for God. Salvation does not rest on human rationalization but on God's revelation.

Peter told Jesus, "You are the Christ, the Son of the living God." And Jesus replied, "Blessed are you...for this was not revealed to you by man, but by my Father in heaven" (Matt. 16:16-17).

Christians are people whose minds have been opened to the truth so that they can receive salvation only as a gift from God. But this is only the beginning. Once we have been given spiritual sight, God wants us to see more and more spiritual reality. That is why Paul prays that God will give the Ephesians "the Spirit of wisdom and revelation" and enlighten the "eyes of [their] hearts" (Eph. 1:17-18).

A Willing Mind

Once saved, some people refuse to allow God to challenge them further. Their problems may concern a personal sin or a particular doctrine. They have fixed opinions and have blocked out any other viewpoint. Such behavior is immature. James tells us that the wisdom from above is "open to reason" and "willing to yield" (3:17, RSV, NKJV). We must listen to the Word, be open to others' opinions and be ready to change our thinking.

A Humble Mind

Although we know that we must not seek the praise of men, we are often in danger of becoming proud of our achievements and spiritual experiences. The Bible warns us, "Do not think of yourself more highly than you ought" (Rom. 12:3), and "in humility consider others better than yourselves" (Phil. 2:3). Jesus, who is "gentle and humble in heart," invites us to "learn from me" (Matt. 11:29).

A Thankful Mind

When we find ourselves in difficult circumstances, we moan almost automatically. As we do this we reinforce negative thinking and become prone to depression and bitterness toward God and others. Paul says, "In all things God works for the good of those who love him" (Rom. 8:28). If we believe this truth, we will live by it and "give thanks in all circumstances" (1 Thess. 5:18).

A Peaceful Mind

We live in an anxious world. On our television screens we seem to see an increasing number of horrendous natural and man-made disasters. Earthquakes, floods, famines and wars wipe out whole cities and leave behind them complete devastation. Closer to home, we have our own personal problems to work out: family, friends, relationships, jobs, sickness — all of these threaten to overwhelm us and create within us a strong tendency to panic.

When Jesus was on earth, He went through extreme pressure yet responded with remarkable calmness. He trusted God, so He experienced "perfect peace" (Is. 26:3). "Do not worry," He said (Matt. 6:25).

Paul adds, "Do not be anxious about anything" (Phil. 4:6). Then we will know His peace in every situation.

The ultimate goal of every Christian is to become more like

Jesus (Rom. 8:29). He did not live at the mercy of wrong thinking. He was not overwhelmed by pressure. Let Him transform your mind, and you will prove His victory in every area of your life.

God wants you to align your thinking with His.

The mind controlled by the Spirit is
life and peace (Rom. 8:6).

You will keep in perfect peace him whose mind
is steadfast, because he trusts in you (Is. 26:3).

We take captive every thought to
make it obedient to Christ (2 Cor. 10:5b).

TWELVE

His Purpose in
Our Generation

*Can you think of a father who has no will or plan for the
life of his son? Can you imagine a man who has no special
desire or pattern in the one he chooses to be his wife?
Can you conceive of a king...who has no will or desire or
law to govern the conduct of his people? A captain who
has no plan for his soldiers? An employer who has no plan
or pattern to guide the labor of his workers? If so, then you
may also think that God does not have a plan for your life,
for every one of these symbols is used in the Bible to
represent the relation the Christian bears to his Lord.[1]*
G. Christian Weiss

Not only does God want us to receive His grace, but He
also wants it to direct the course of our lives. It is an
ongoing process. Grace brings us safe thus far, and
grace leads us home.

We Have a Free Will

Christians are not programmed people. The good Shepherd
does not point a remote-control handset at one of His sheep and
transmit His orders into its mind! His desire is for relationship,
so He gives us the will to choose how closely we live to Him.
Christians are not sheep without a Shepherd — but some of
them have a tendency to wander away from the protection that
the Shepherd offers. They are the laid-back believers who ap-
pear outwardly committed but are not particularly enthusiastic

58

about giving their lives wholly to God. Instead, they simply drift about the field, nibble at Christian teaching here and there and spend more time with the flock than with the Shepherd.

If you live out of earshot of the Shepherd on a daily basis, you will find it hard to hear Him when you suddenly want to know His will over a major issue. Panic-stricken, you will exclaim, "What does God want me to do?" And a confident decision which could have been born out of much practice at hearing God is, instead, the product of a lot of sleepless nights.

God Has a Will

The world is not a programmed planet. God has not wound it up and abandoned it. He is active throughout history: planning, motivating and working out everything "in conformity with the purpose of his will" (Eph. 1:11b). What He says, He does. He is never taken off guard, and nothing happens without His knowledge or consent. When we know that God is in control, we can trust Him in all sorts of puzzling circumstances.

God Has a Will for Us

God's plan for you began before you were born. He decided that He wanted you on the earth, put you in a family and knew exactly what would happen to you. He saved you, and now He wants to continue the plans He has for you. You may be focusing on how unqualified you are.

You are not useless to God, because God does not create useless things. If you feel that God will not use you because of something you have done, remember that Moses savagely murdered an Egyptian, that Peter fervently denied Jesus and that Paul brutally persecuted believers. If they had thought that God wouldn't use them, where would the church be today? God knows your weaknesses, but He still wants you to fit into the plan that He has worked out for your life since the beginning of time. God is looking at His Son's righteousness in you and is excited about what He is going to do with your life.

God Wants Us to Know His Will

Paul urges us to "not be foolish, but understand what the Lord's will is" (Eph. 5:17). God does not expect us to wander around aimlessly, guessing what He has planned for us. But neither does He want us to seek His will in minute detail.

Jesus knew that the Spirit had anointed Him to preach and heal (Luke 4:18-19), but He may not have been aware of His exact itinerary. God has appointed us to do a specific work and is anxious for us to discover the general direction of that calling. If we offer our bodies to God and allow Him to transform us by renewing our minds, we "will be able to test and approve what God's will is" (Rom. 12:2b). We give God our bodies and minds, and He reveals His will to us.

Serving God's Purpose

Before his coronation King Saul seemed eager to do God's will. But he disobeyed God and lost the throne to David, his successor. Unlike Saul, David fulfilled his calling. Before he died he had "served God's purpose in his own generation" (Acts 13:36). King Jesus said, "I have come down from heaven not to do my will but to do the will of him who sent me" (John 6:38). He knew that He had to die for the sins of the world. At the end of His life He declared to His Father, "I have brought you glory on earth by completing the work you gave me to do" (John 17:4). And on the cross He cried, "It is finished" (John 19:30).

We were born to serve God's purpose in our generation. We can choose to live in the past, assuming that God will work in the same way as He has always done. Or we can set our sails to the present-day move of the Spirit and be open to new waves of blessing. Some Christians think that God's will is "important, burdensome and necessary." The Bible says that it is "good, pleasing and perfect" (Rom. 12:2b). A good human father wants his children to enjoy their work. God is no different. He gave His Son a task and anointed Him with the "oil of joy" (Heb. 1:9b) to accomplish it.

Jesus willingly submitted to God's will because, unlike Eve, He knew it could not be bettered. It was nourishing enough for Him to call it His "food" (John 4:34). The only way to discover if God's will is good, pleasing and perfect is to devote yourself to it. You will find it tough at times. God will test you in some fiery situations, but if you trust Him, He will bring you forth as gold (Job 23:10).

At the end of your life God wants you to know the tremendous satisfaction of having done His will. He longs to hear you declare, "I have fought the good fight, I have finished the race, I have kept the faith" (2 Tim. 4:7). And He looks forward to welcoming you into heaven with the words, "Well done, good and faithful servant! ...Come and share your master's happiness!" (Matt. 25:21).

Blessed is the man who finds out which way God is moving and then gets going in the same direction.
Anonymous

God has a plan for your life.

For I know the plans I have for you, declares the Lord, plans to prosper you and not to harm you, plans to give you hope and a future (Jer. 29:11).

Trust in the Lord with all your heart and lean not on your own understanding; in all your ways acknowledge him, and he will make your paths straight (Prov. 3:5-6).

NOTES

Chapter 1

1. Steven Brown, *When Being Good Isn't Good Enough* (Cambridge, England: Crossway Books, 1990), p. 57.

Chapter 2

1. Martyn Lloyd-Jones, *Romans 7:1-8:4*, (Edinburgh, Scotland: Banner of Truth Trust, 1973), p. 49.

Chapter 4

1. George Sweeting, comp., *Great Quotes and Illustrations* (Milton Keynes, England: Word Books, 1985), p. 92.
2. *Ibid.*, p. 22.

Chapter 5

1. John Murray, *The New International Commentary on the New Testament, Epistle to the Romans* (Grand Rapids, Mich.: Wm. B. Eerdmans, 1968), p. 347.
2. Lloyd-Jones, *Romans 7:1-8:4* , pp. 271-272.

Chapter 6

1. Sweeting, comp., *Great Quotes,* p. 168.

Chapter 7

1. Charles R. Swindoll, *The Grace Awakening* (Milton Keynes, England: Word Books, 1990), p. 117.
2. Watchman Nee, *The Normal Christian Life*, (Eastbourne, England: Kingsway Publications, 1961), pp. 45-46.

Notes

Chapter 8

1. Sweeting, *Great Quotes*, p. 246.
2. *Ibid.*, p. 255.

Chapter 9

1. Richard Shelley Taylor, *The Disciplined Life*, (Minneapolis, Minn.: Bethany House, 1962), p. 23.

Chapter 10

1. Sweeting, *Great Quotes*, p. 267.

Chapter 11

1. A. W. Tozer, *The Best of A. W. Tozer,* (Grand Rapids, Mich.: Baker Book House, 1978), *pp. 45-46.*

Chapter 12

1. Sweeting, *Great Quotes*, p. 128.

CHRISTIAN LIFE BOOKS
TOOLS FOR SPIRIT-LED LIVING

If you enjoyed *God's Amazing Grace*, we would like to recommend the following books:

Effective Prayer
by John Dawson, B. J. Willhite, Francis MacNutt, Judson Cornwall and Larry Lea

The Gifts of the Spirit
by Jack Hayford, John Wimber, Reinhard Bonnke, Judith MacNutt, Michael P. Williams, Mark A. Pearson, John Archer and Mahesh Chavda

Miracles Never Cease!
by William DeArteaga, Paul Thigpen, Jack Deere and Oral Roberts

Prophecy in the Church
by Martin Scott

God's Remedy for Rejection
by Derek Prince

Parents and Teachers: Equipping the Younger Saints
by David Walters

Living in the Supernatural
by Kathie Walters

Healing
by Charles & Frances Hunter

Available at your local Christian bookstore or from:

Creation House
600 Rinehart Road
Lake Mary, FL 32746
1-800-451-4598